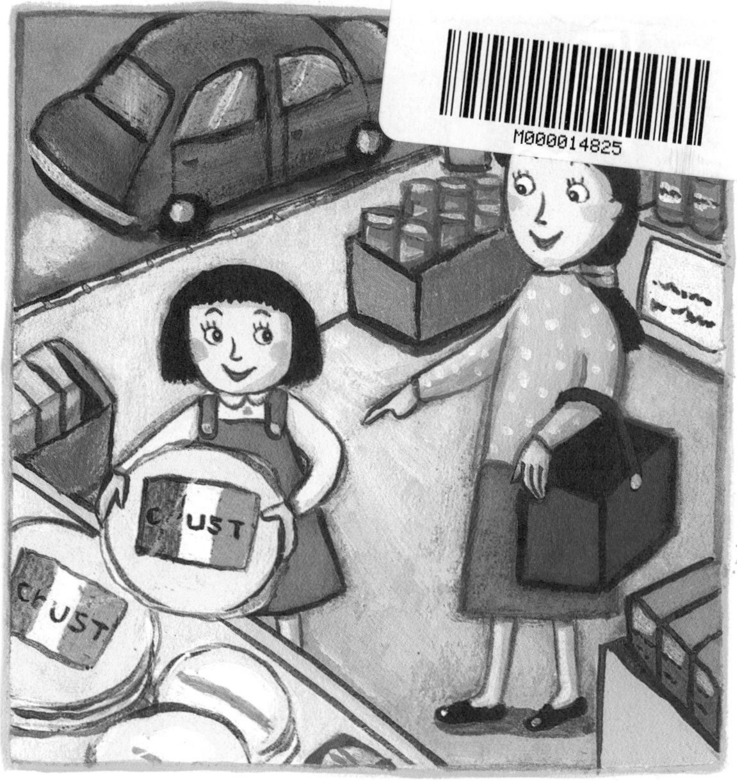

We get a crust.

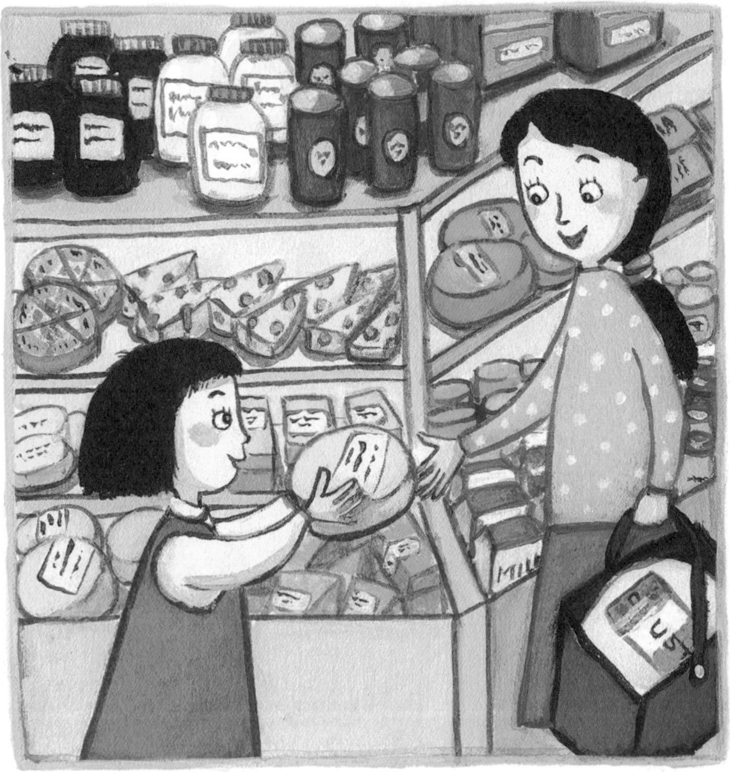

We get cheese.

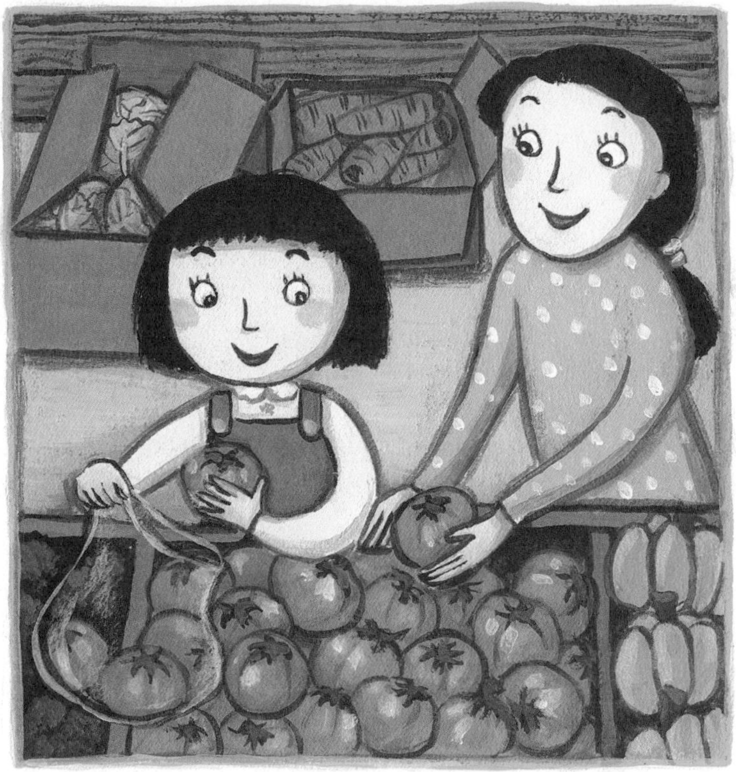

We get tomatoes.

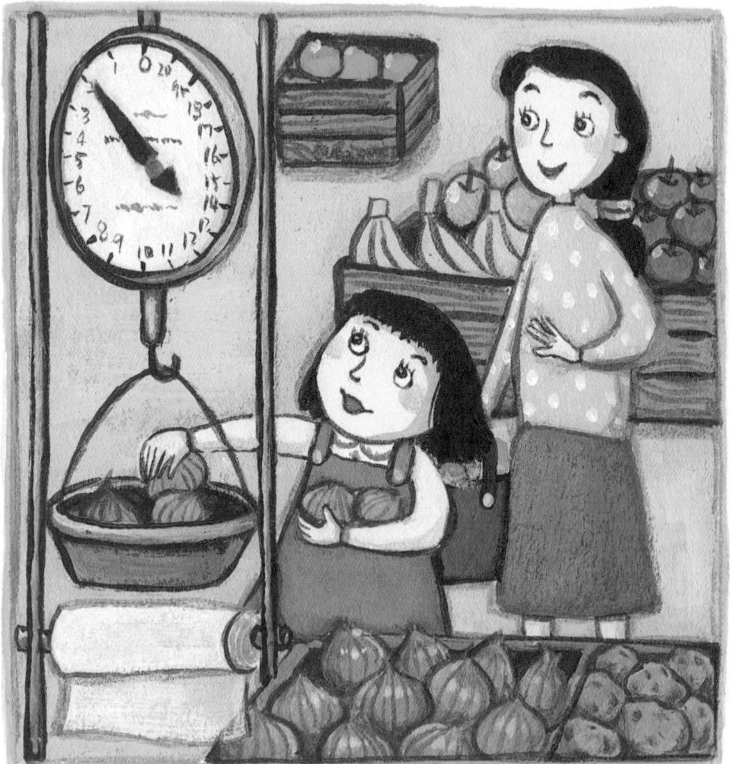

We get onions.

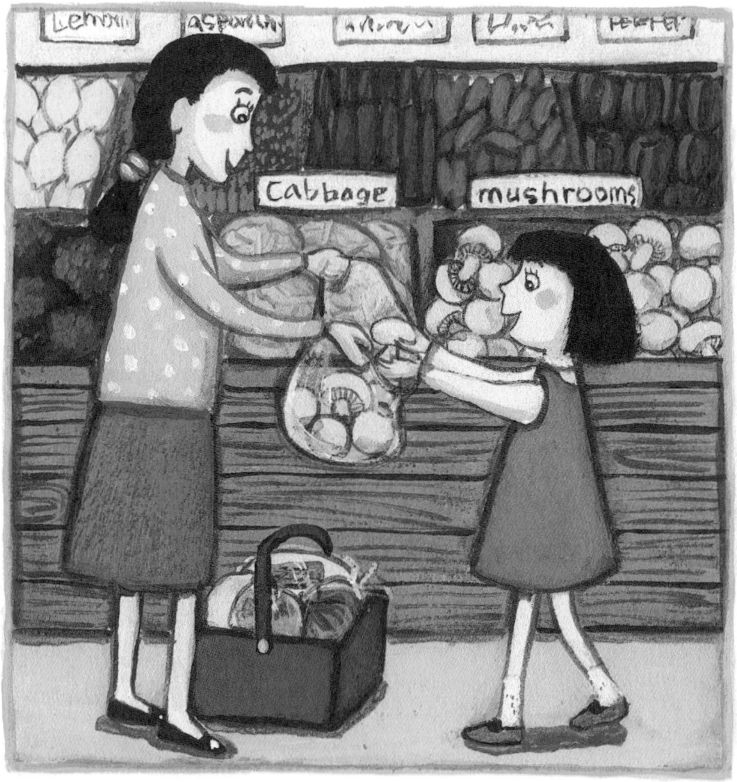

We get mushrooms.

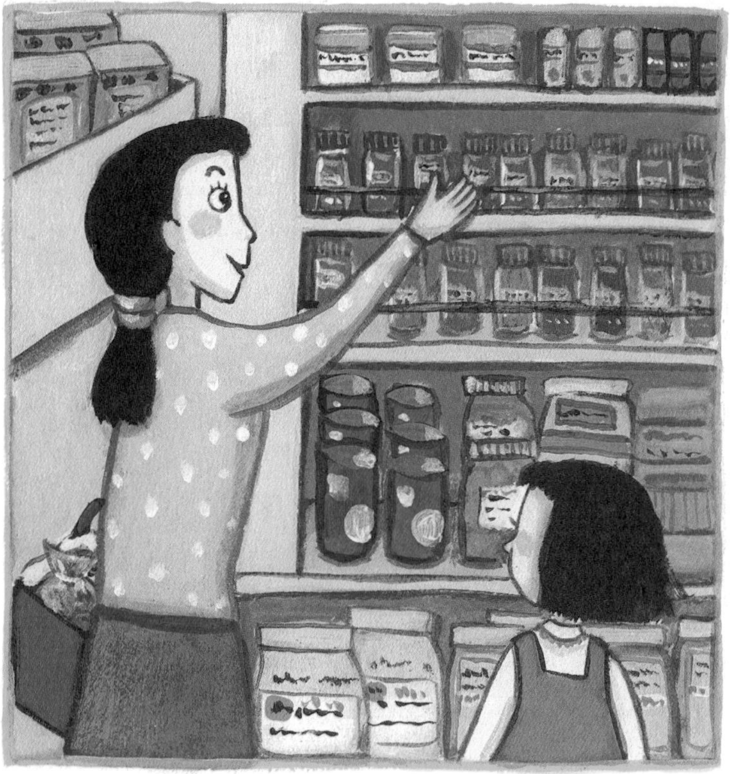

We get spices.

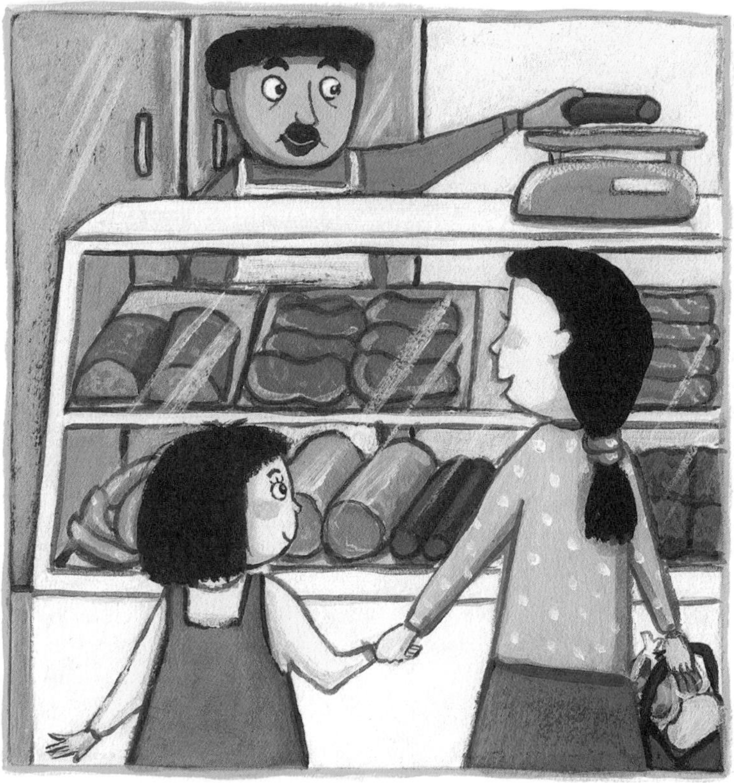

We get pepperoni.

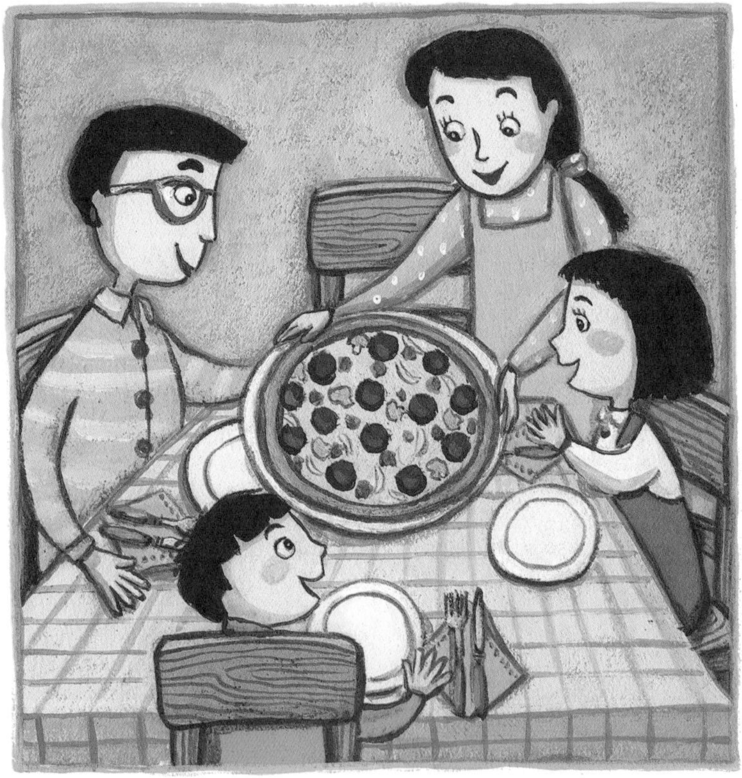

We get pizza!